# A Look at Kenya

## by Helen Frost

Consulting Editor: Gail Saunders-Smith, Ph.D.

Consultant: Lynette Jackson, Ph.D.
Assistant Professor of African History
Barnard College/Columbia University
New York City

## Pebble Books

an imprint of Capstone Press
Mankato, Minnesota

Pebble Books are published by Capstone Press
151 Good Counsel Drive, P.O. Box 669, Mankato, Minnesota 56002
www.capstonepub.com

Books published by Capstone Press are manufactured with paper
containing at least 10 percent post-consumer waste.

*Library of Congress Cataloging-in-Publication Data*
Frost, Helen, 1949–
    A look at Kenya / by Helen Frost.
    p. cm.—(Our world)
    Includes bibliographical references and index.
    ISBN-13: 978-0-7368-0984-9 (hardcover)
    ISBN-10: 0-7368-0984-8 (hardcover)
    ISBN-13: 978-0-7368-4853-4 (softcover pbk.)
    ISBN-10: 0-7368-4853-3 (softcover pbk.)
    1. Kenya—Juvenile literature. [1. Kenya.] I. Title. II. Series: Our world (Pebble
Books)
DT433.522.F76 2002
967.62—dc21                                     00-012779

Summary: Simple text and photographs depict the land, animals, and people
of Kenya.

## Note to Parents and Teachers

The Our World series supports national social studies standards related to
culture. This book describes and illustrates the land, animals, and people
of Kenya. The photographs support early readers in understanding the
text. The repetition of words and phrases helps early readers learn new
words. This book also introduces early readers to subject-specific
vocabulary words, which are defined in the Words to Know section. Early
readers may need assistance to read some words and to use the Table of
Contents, Words to Know, Read More, Internet Sites, and Index/Word List
sections of the book.

Printed in the United States of America in Stevens Point, Wisconsin.
082013    007666R

# Table of Contents

# Kenya

★ Nairobi

Kenya is on the east coast of Africa. The capital of Kenya is Nairobi. Nairobi is the largest city in Kenya.

Kenya's flag

Kenya is warmest near the coast. Kenya is cooler in the mountains. Kenya has a rainy season and a dry season.

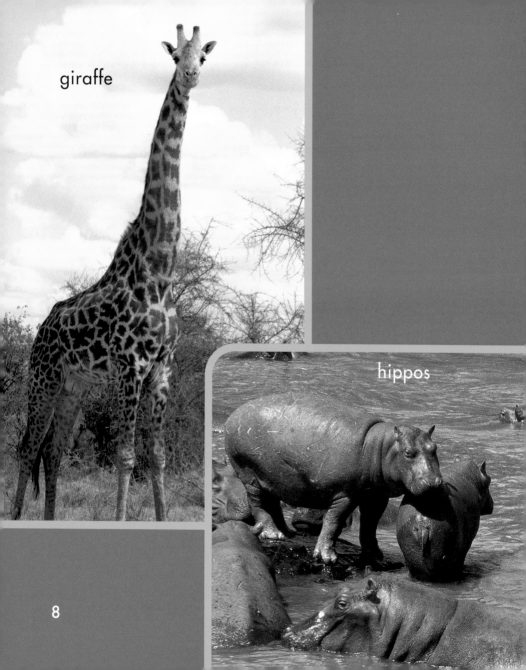

giraffe

hippos

8

Giraffes, elephants, lions, and zebras live on Kenya's savannas. Hippos and crocodiles live in Kenya's rivers.

More than 30 million
people live in Kenya.
Some Kenyans live
in cities. Most Kenyans
live in the country.

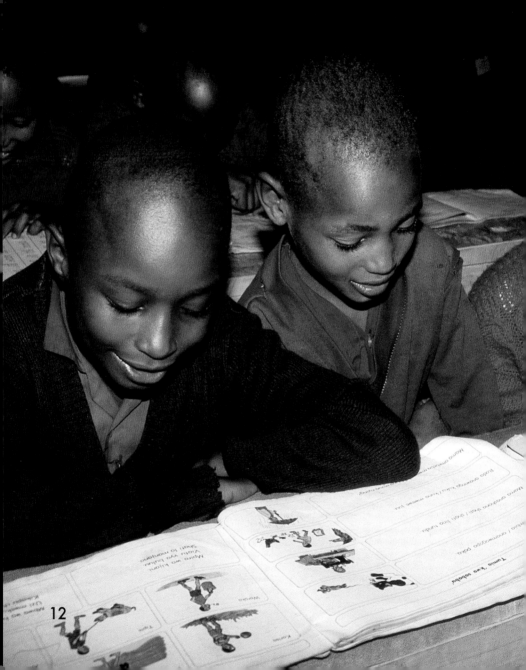

Kiswahili and English are Kenya's official languages. Students learn both languages in school.

Some Kenyans like to run. Runners from Kenya have won races all around the world. Kenyans also like to play soccer.

Some Kenyans fish or guide tourists to earn money. Some Kenyan farmers grow coffee, tea, and sugarcane.

Kenya's money is counted in shillings.

18

Some Kenyans have cars.
Most Kenyans walk, run,
or take a bus.

Scientists have found very old human bones in Kenya. They think that the world's first people may have lived in Kenya.

# Words to Know

**Africa**—one of the seven continents of the world; Africa is located between the Atlantic Ocean and the Indian Ocean.

**capital**—the city in a country where the government is based; the capital of Kenya is Nairobi.

**Kiswahili**—one of Kenya's official languages; many other languages are also spoken in Kenya.

**savanna**—a flat, grassy plain; many wild animals and birds live on Kenya's savannas.

**shilling**—the money used in Kenya; shillings are also used in other countries; the shilling in Kenya is called the Kenyan shilling (KSh).

**tourist**—someone who travels and visits places for fun, relaxation, or adventure

# Read More

**Dahl, Michael.** *Kenya.* Countries of the World. Mankato, Minn.: Bridgestone Books, 1997.

**Gresko, Marcia S.** *Kenya.* Letters Home From. Woodbridge, Conn.: Blackbirch Press, 1999.

**McCollum, Sean.** *Kenya.* Globetrotters Club. Minneapolis: Carolrhoda Books, 1999.

**Ryan, Patrick.** *Kenya.* Faces and Places. Chanhassen, Minn.: Child's World, 1999.

# Internet Sites

FactHound offers a safe, fun way to find Internet sites related to this book. All of the sites on FactHound have been researched by our staff.

Here's all you do:

Visit *www.facthound.com*

**FactHound will fetch the best sites for you!**

# Index/Word List

Africa, 5
bones, 21
city, 5, 11
coast, 5, 7
country, 11
crocodiles, 9
elephants, 9
English, 13
farmers, 17

giraffes, 9
hippos, 9
Kenyans, 11, 15, 17, 19
Kiswahili, 13
languages, 13
lions, 9
money, 17
mountains, 7

Nairobi, 5
people, 11, 21
rivers, 9
savannas, 9
scientists, 21
tourists, 17
world, 15
zebras, 9

**Word Count: 161**
**Early-Intervention Level: 18**

**Editorial Credits**
Mari C. Schuh, editor; Kia Bielke, cover designer and illustrator; Kimberly Danger, photo researcher

**Photo Credits**
Bettmann/CORBIS, 20
Corel, 8 (left)
Michele Burgess, cover, 12
Photo Network/Howard Folsom, 10
Photri-Microstock, 16
Pictor/Paul Conklin, 18
Stan Osolinski/Root Resources, 1
Trip/W. Jacobs, 6 (top)
Unicorn Stock Photos/Rod Furgason, 6 (bottom)
Visuals Unlimited/Barbara Gerlach, 8 (right)
Yann Arthus-Bertrand/CORBIS, 14

The author thanks the children's section staff at the Allen County Public Library in Fort Wayne, Indiana, for research assistance.